Reflecting
The
Glory

Reflecting The Glory

by Ruth Rieder

Sequel to:
Power Before
The Throne

Reflecting The Glory

Copyright © 2000
Ruth Rieder

All artwork drawn by Wade Plemons

*Unless otherwise indicated, all Scripture quotations are taken
from the King James Version of the Bible.*

ISBN: 0-9674360-2-8
First printing: August 2000–5,000 copies

FOR INFORMATION CONTACT:
Ruth Rieder
P. O. Box 15252
Rio Rancho, NM 87174

Printed in the United States by
Morris Publishing
3212 E. Hwy 30
Kearney, NE 68847
1-800-650-7888

Dedicated to my sister, Beth Burns, who is a true reflection of the glory of God in this dark world. Your love for God has inspired and enriched my life. May you continue to shine as a beacon of light, reflecting the image of Jesus.

Acknowledgments

Words cannot express the deep adoration and love I feel for my Lord and Master, Jesus Christ. *"I rejoice at thy word, as one that findeth great spoil."* My heart's desire is to know You more intimately through the revelation of Your Word and the communion of prayer. May my life reflect Your glory!

MY BELOVED HUSBAND: Thank you for all you have invested in my life. You have opened my understanding into the deep things of the Spirit through your anointed teaching and preaching. I love you, darling!

MY PRECIOUS DAUGHTERS, Angelica and Miriam: You breathe life into our home with all your delightful ways. I will never cease to thank the Lord for bringing both of you into our lives. May your lives always reflect God's glory. I love you!

DONNA TEN EYCK: You have given me the priceless treasure of loyal and unfailing friendship. *"Iron sharpeneth iron; so a man sharpeneth the countenance of his friend."* I thank God for the wellspring of wisdom that He has placed within you. It has been a flowing brook of refreshment in my life. Thank you for the *hours* invested in this book and for being my "Armor Bearer"!

JOAN PIERCE: Thank you for lending your skills in English and editing to perfect this manuscript. You continually challenge me to hone my writing skills. Thank you for encouraging me in the pursuit of excellence. I treasure your friendship and love.

WADE PLEMONS: Thank you for another job well done. Your artwork conveys the message of the book before one word has been read. May the anointing of the Lord continue to rest upon your creative ministry.

BETHANY SLEDGE: I thank the Lord for allowing our paths to cross so we can join our skills to minister through the printed word. Thank you for bringing this manuscript to completion.

Table of Contents

Introduction

W hen *Power Before The Throne* was released in the spring of 1999, I never dreamed it would impact so many in such a short span of time. Without a doubt this is the Lord's doing, and it is marvelous in my eyes. *Reflecting The Glory* continues the exploration into the positive power of holiness which began in my previous book. This sequel offers sound Scriptural support for adhering to God's standard of righteousness.

When the eyes of our understanding are enlightened, we are able to comprehend more completely the glorious privilege of being a child of God. As the light of revelation penetrates our souls, it causes the shadowy, gray areas to dissipate. The end result being vessels *"unto honour, sanctified, and meet for the master's use, and prepared unto every good work."* Let us *"walk in the light, as he is in the light,"* for *"God is light, and in him is no darkness at all."* Truly we are the reflection of God's glory in the midst of a world ruled by darkness.

God's Gold

"There's gold in them thar hills!"

This proclamation sent thousands of people on the world's largest treasure hunt. One of them was a lanky, young prospector named George Jackson. On January 6, 1859, he found himself dangerously short of food in the snowy Rockies thirty miles west of Denver. Jackson had just decided to quit his gold hunting and to head toward Denver when he chanced upon hot, mineral springs near Clear Creek. There he saw–as he related in his diary–"hundreds of beautiful mountain sheep, great big bucks with curled horns, all grazing about the springs where the warm vapors had melted the snow and left the grass for them to nibble at." Jackson shot a buck and cut chops for himself and his two dogs. Then, encouraged by the hearty meal and a new food supply, he made a momentous decision: he would devote one more day to his hunt for gold.

Next morning, Jackson resumed his search along the south fork of Clear Creek. Late in the day he spotted a promising gravel bar. Building a large bonfire to thaw the surface, he hacked out some slushy sand with his belt knife and panned it in his tin drinking cup. He swished water in the cup until all the light sand had washed away. A few tiny but heavy, yellow flakes remained in the cup. GOLD!

Eagerly Jackson panned several more handfuls of sand, collecting a vial of gold dust and one small nugget. The gold weighed about one ounce and was worth ten dollars at the current price in Denver. He went to bed that night dreaming of riches galore, a fine house, good clothes, a carriage, horses, travel, and so much more.

Jackson had discovered the first major gold field in the West's immense interior wilderness. When news of his find burst upon Denver, the results were immediate and profound. The headlines began to scream: "The New El Dorado!!! Gold in Kansas territory!"

By April, 1859, a torrent of prospectors–estimated at 100,000–had set out for the "New El Dorado". Most of them were ill equipped and ignorant of the hazards that lay ahead. Their wagons, painted with the slogan "Pike's Peak or Bust," broke down in the prairie. Many "fifty-niners" got lost or perished of thirst, hunger, and disease. Hostile

Plains Indians waylaid some. About half the emigrants never reached the Rockies while others turned back, bitterly crying, "Fraud!" after a cursory look failed to reveal any bonanzas.

Meanwhile, Jackson and his partners continued panning for gold. Each week they were extracting nearly two thousand dollars' worth of gold from the south fork of Clear Creek. News spread like wildfire as Jackson's strike launched a gold rush that opened a new saga in western mining. Prospector William Parsons described it as a mad, furious race for wealth, in which men almost lost their identity as they toiled, wrestled, and lived a fierce, riotous, wearing albeit exciting life. They forgot home and kindred, abandoned old, steady habits, and were filled with restlessness. These miners were a hearty breed given to impulsive generosity and lavish ways.

The fabulous Comstock Lode, discovered June, 1859, in the Washoe Mountains of Nevada, yielded $400 million in silver and gold over three decades. However, this vast wealth was acquired with great sacrifice and under horrific working conditions. An editor named William Wright described the working environment within the mines as follows:

Candles and lamps burned everywhere, 24 hours a

day. The temperature at 1,500 feet was over 100 degrees. In that heat miners wore breechcloths or long underwear bottoms cut off at mid-thigh. To keep dirt out of their hair, miners wore a head covering: narrow-brimmed hats or felt skullcaps cut from ordinary hats. To protect their feet from sharp quartz they wore shoes. That was the extent of their safety equipment.

At the depth of 1,500 to 2,000 feet the rock was so hot it was painful to the naked hand. In many places, from crevices in the rock or from holes drilled into it, streams of hot water gush out. In these places the thermometer often shows a temperature of 120 to 130 degrees. It is as hot as in the hottest Turkish bath. To make it possible for men to work, great blowers on the surface forced cool air into the mine through pipes two feet in diameter. Despite this, the men could only work a half an hour at a time and then had to rest for half an hour. While resting, each man drank several pints of water and chewed ice, placed in barrels near the tubes of the blowers. In one mine, the Consolidated Virginia, about a ton and a half of ice was lowered to the men each day. When their rest period was over, the men walked back to their jobs carrying fast melting lumps of ice in both hands.

However beautiful the candlelit ore may have

appeared to outsiders, it was extracted at great human cost. Possibly ten thousand men all told worked on the Comstock at one time or another. At least three hundred of them were killed and six hundred maimed or crippled. There were periods when a man was killed every week and others grievously injured every day. Falls were the most common cause of death. Miners were also killed in cave-ins and underground fires. In spite of the hazards involved, men persisted in their quest for riches. No price seemed too great to pay. When they struck pay dirt, all sacrifices paled by comparison.

Millions and maybe even billions of dollars in the form of gold and silver were extracted from the creeks, rivers, hills, and mountains of the American West. In Dakota's Black Hills in 1859, a prospector named Moses Manuel and his brother Fred found the Homestake mine. This was probably the richest single mine in the world with an output that eventually reached one billion dollars. Perhaps the densest concentration of gold ever located was discovered in 1890 at Cripple Creek, Colorado. In an area six miles square, 475 mines produced $350 million in twenty-five years.

The most sensational find of that period, and perhaps of all time, was made in Cripple Creek, Colorado, during 1914. Dick Roelofs, a mining engineer at the Cresson mine, had been working with a crew in a tunnel 1,200 feet underground. They were cutting their way along a good lode when they suddenly holed through hard rock into a cavity, technically known as a geode but usually called a "vug" in miners' lingo. This was the biggest, richest vug Roelofs had ever seen, and the discovery threw him into a tizzy. After glancing through the opening with his miner's lamp, he sent his men to fetch an ironworker, who installed a vault door barring the way into the vug. Armed guards were posted at the door.

To keep everything aboveboard, Roelofs rounded up two trustworthy witnesses. The trio descended the Cresson's shaft. Roelofs led the way to the steel door and opened it.

The men stepped into a wonderland of solid gold. The vug was twenty feet long, fifteen feet wide, and forty feet high. Its walls blazed with millions of gold crystals and 24-carat flakes as big as a thumbnail. Pure gold boulders littered the floor amid piles of white quartz like spun glass.

One of Roelofs' witnesses hazarded a hoarse guess; the wall surfaces alone might be worth $100,000. He had underestimated by more than three hundred percent. After

Roelof's trusted miners had scraped the walls and filled 1,400 sacks with crystals and flakes, the lot sold for $378,000. One thousand sacks of lower grade ore brought $90,000 more. Then the crew mined the outer layers of rock–ore worth more than $700,000. The vug was stripped in four weeks, and it enriched the mine owners by the sum of $1,200,000.

Dreamlike wealth and beauty such as this drove miners to delve into the earth. Gold was the glamour metal of the pioneer epoch, the main chance and chief attraction for every man who ventured forth in hopes of striking it rich.[1]

When God created valuable metals such as silver and gold, He placed them deep in the heart of the earth. They can only be obtained through perseverance and intensive, backbreaking labor. Correspondingly, the precious truths of God's Word do not lie on the surface for the halfhearted soul to pick up casually and toss aside. These treasures are only imparted to those who set themselves to know the One *"in whom are hid all the treasures of wisdom and knowledge."*[2] To find Him you must seek for Him with all your heart. An intense pursuit of God is the earmark of a wise and prudent person. *"The heart of the prudent getteth knowledge; and the ear of the wise seeketh knowledge. "[3]*

In one of his dialogues, Job depicts man's intense pursuit of wealth in the depths of the earth. *"There is a mine for silver and a place where gold is refined. Iron is taken from the earth, and copper is smelted from ore. Man puts an end to the darkness; he searches the farthest recesses for ore in the blackest darkness. Far from where people dwell he cuts a shaft, in places forgotten by the foot of man; far from men he dangles and sways. The earth, from which food comes, is transformed below as by fire; sapphires come from its rocks, and its dust contains nuggets of gold. No bird of prey knows that hidden path, no falcon's eye has seen it. Proud beasts do not set foot on it, and no lion prowls there. Man's hand assaults the flinty rock and lays bare the roots of the mountains. He tunnels through the rock; his eyes see all its treasures. He searches the sources of the rivers and brings hidden things to light."*

At this point in his discourse, Job pauses to ask two very important questions, *"But where can wisdom be found? Where does understanding dwell?"* Although mankind will go to great lengths in order to obtain earthly treasures, does anyone want to seek for the true riches? How valuable are wisdom and understanding? Are they worth the investment of time and energy?

"Man does not comprehend its worth; it cannot be found in the land of the living. The deep says, 'It is not in me'; the sea says, 'It is not with me.' It cannot be bought with the gold of Ophir, with precious onyx or sapphires. Neither gold nor crystal can compare with it, nor can it be had for jewels of gold. Coral and jasper are not worthy of mention; the price of wisdom is beyond rubies. The topaz of Cush cannot compare with it; it cannot be bought with pure gold."

After describing the incredible value of wisdom, Job inquires once more, *"Where then does wisdom come from? Where does understanding dwell? It is hidden from the eyes of every living thing, concealed even from the birds of the air. Destruction and Death say, 'Only a rumor of it has reached our ears.'"*

Does anyone know the way to this treasure trove? *"<u>God understands the way to it and he alone knows where it dwells</u>, for he views the ends of the earth and sees everything under the heavens. When he established the force of the wind and measured out the waters, when he made a decree for the rain and a path for the thunderstorm, then he looked at wisdom and appraised it; he confirmed it and tested it. And he said unto man, 'THE*

FEAR OF THE LORD–THAT IS WISDOM, AND TO SHUN EVIL IS UNDERSTANDING. "[4]

The holiness questions that confront the modern day Church are no surprise to God because He knows the end from the beginning. All the answers are contained in His Word; however, it will take time, effort, and sacrifice to extract them from God's gold mine. It will be necessary to dig deeply for these riches.

The wise man Solomon said to cry after knowledge and lift up your voice for understanding. We are to seek her as silver and search as for hid treasure. *"**Then** shalt thou understand the fear of the LORD, and find the knowledge of God. For the LORD giveth wisdom: out of his mouth cometh knowledge and understanding."*[5]

Many wonderful spiritual truths have already been discovered through the years. Each new insight found within the pages of Scripture has caused us to *"rejoice at thy word, as one that findeth great spoil."*[6] Still, God's gold supply remains inexhaustible. His wisdom is boundless; His *"commandment is exceeding broad."*[7]

"O the depth of the riches both of the wisdom and knowledge of God! how unsearchable are his judgments, and his ways past finding out! For who hath known the mind of the Lord? or who hath been his counsellor? Or

who hath first given to him, and it shall be recompensed unto him again? For of him, and through him, and to him, are all things: to whom be glory for ever. Amen.[8]

Gold is found anywhere you stick your shovel, so let's dig deeply and go after **GOD'S GOLD!!**

Chapter One Footnotes:

1. All mining information and quotes excerpted from: Time Life Books, *The Old West, The Miners* (Time Inc., 1976).

2. Colossians 2:3

3. Proverbs 18:15

4. Job 28, New International Version

5. Proverbs 2:3-6

6. Psalm 119:162

7. Psalm 119:96

8. Romans 11:33-36

"Son of the Morning"

I n our study let us travel back to the dawn of time. At the beginning all that existed was God. He referred to Himself as the "I Am." *"Thus saith the LORD the King of Israel, and his redeemer the LORD of hosts; <u>I am the first, and I am the last</u>; and beside me there is no God. Remember the former things of old: for I am God, and there is none else; I am God, and there is none like me, declaring the end from the beginning, and from ancient times the things that are not yet done, saying, My counsel shall stand, and I will do all my pleasure. "*[1]

Throughout Scripture we are allowed to catch minute glimpses into the eternal realm. Behind the scenes of our physical existence is a very real spirit world. What transpires on earth is simply a reflection of unseen spiritual activity. *"While we look not at the things which are seen, but at the things which are not seen: for the things which are seen are temporal; but the things which are not seen are eternal.*"[2]

As God set His divine plan in motion, He fashioned spirit-beings, called "angels". The *"sons of God"* were present and *"shouted for joy"* when God created the heavens and the earth.[3] Job 1:6 and 2:1 clarify the *"sons of God"* are the heavenly host. The Word of God identifies three angels by name, Gabriel, Michael, and Lucifer. They were created to fill specific roles in the heavenly domain.

Gabriel is a leading angel whose name first appears in the book of Daniel. His name literally means "Mighty one of God" or "God has shown Himself mighty." As God's messenger, his assignment was to give *"skill and understanding"* to Daniel.[4]

In the first chapter of Luke, we see Gabriel at work again, bringing a message of hope to Zacharias. Elisabeth would bear him a son whose name would be called John. This child coming in the spirit and power of Elias would be great in the sight of the Lord. Six months later Gabriel appeared to Mary, saying, *"Fear not, Mary: for thou hast found favour with God. And, behold, thou shalt conceive in thy womb, and bring forth a son, and shalt call his name JESUS."*[5]

Another angel mentioned in Scripture is Michael, whose name means "like God." The tenth chapter of Daniel gives us a rare glimpse into the spiritual warfare that takes place behind the scenes. For twenty-one days Daniel sought for understanding of a vision through prayer and fasting. From the first day that Daniel sought the Lord, an angel attempted to bring spiritual enlightenment to him. However, the messenger met with resistance from the prince of the kingdom of Persia. This battle lasted for three weeks until Michael, one of the chief princes, came to intervene. His prowess as a warrior enabled the angel to break through to Daniel. The angel informed Daniel that the conflict would only intensify when he returned to fight with Michael against the prince of Persia, as well as the prince of Grecia.

Further evidence of this archangel's abilities is found in the book of Jude as Michael contended with the devil concerning the body of Moses. Revelation records another spiritual conflict when Michael and his angels fought against the dragon and his angels. During the war in heaven, the archangel and his army prevailed, and the great dragon was cast out.[6] Each encounter with Michael throughout Holy Writ portrays him as a triumphant warrior Prince.

The third angel identified in the Bible is Lucifer. His name means "son of the morning" or literally "day star or morning star". According to the Hebrew, this name refers to his brightness.[7] Lucifer was created with musical ability, and his outward appearance differed from all other angelic creatures. No other angel could compare to Lucifer, who was created *"full of wisdom, and perfect in beauty."*[8]

Ezekiel 28 describes his magnificent appearance in detail. *"Thou hast been in Eden the garden of God; every precious stone was thy covering, the sardius, topaz, and the diamond, the beryl, the onyx, and the jasper, the sapphire, the emerald, and the carbuncle, and gold: the workmanship of thy tabrets and of thy pipes was prepared in thee in the day that thou wast created."*[9]

Why did God create him in this manner? If Gabriel is the messenger and Michael is the warrior, what was Lucifer's role? Is there a specific reason that God gave him a jeweled covering unlike all the other angels? The answers to these questions can be found within the pages of God's Word.

In the pursuit of understanding, focusing on the true nature and manifestation of God is imperative. Because we are finite creatures, encapsulated within the temporal world, we seek to understand the spirit realm from this point of reference. So often God is pictured in human form sitting on a throne in heaven; however, John wrote, *"God is a Spirit."*[10]

When Moses desired to see the glory of God, the Lord told him, *"Thou canst not see my face: for there shall no man see me, and live."*[11] Jesus told His disciples, *"A spirit hath not flesh and bones, as ye see me have."*[12] During a discourse with the Jews, Jesus informed them that they had never heard God's voice at any time nor had seen His shape.[13] John recorded in his gospel, *"No man hath seen God at any time."*[14] Paul said, *"No man hath seen [Him], nor can see [Him]."*[15]

The wise king Solomon stated in his prayer of dedication, *"But will God in very deed dwell with men on the earth? behold, heaven and the heaven of heavens cannot contain thee; how much less this house which I have built!"*[16] Upon examining these Scriptures, we see that the essence of God is Spirit, and He fills all known expanse, *"For in him we live, and move, and have our being; as certain also of your own poets have said, For we are also his offspring."*[17]

Although God is Spirit, He manifests His glory in a distinct fashion. David said, *"Bless the LORD, O my soul.*

O LORD my God, thou art very great; thou art clothed with honour and majesty. <u>Who coverest thyself with light as with a garment.</u>[18] The apostle John declared, *"This then is the message which we have heard of him, and declare unto you, that <u>GOD IS LIGHT</u>, and in him is no darkness at all."*[19] Paul stated that He dwells *"in the light which no man can approach unto."*[20]

Exodus 24:17 describes the glory of the Lord as a devouring fire on the top of Mount Sinai. Fire is a form of light. When Paul encountered the Lord on the road to Damascus, a light from heaven shone around him.[21] As Paul recounted his testimony before the Jews in Acts 22, he said, *"I could not see for the glory of the light."* Finally, in his description of the New Jerusalem, John the Revelator wrote, *"And the city had no need of the sun, neither of the moon, to shine in it: <u>for the glory of God did lighten it</u>, and the Lamb is the light thereof."*[22]

This brings us back to our study of why Lucifer was created in such a unique manner. God is Spirit, and He manifests His glory in the form of light. Herein lies the key to understanding Lucifer's role. From the beginning, Lucifer was created with the ability to praise God through his skillfulness in music. As Heaven's worship leader, he ministered before the Lord in the midst of the stones of fire. The strains of skillful music resounding through the heavenly realm would invoke the manifestation of God's glory. When the light of God's glory descended, it came in contact with Lucifer's jeweled covering, resulting in a kaleidoscope of brilliant color. What an awesome sight it must have been to see the most beautiful creature ever created reflecting the glory of the Lord as he ministered in worship before the throne of God!

This position of high honor was also linked to a grave responsibility. Ezekiel called Lucifer the ***"anointed cherub that covereth"*** and the ***"covering cherub."***[23] The word for "covereth" and "covering" in the Hebrew is **"sakak"** (pronounced *saw–kak'*). It means "to fence in, cover over, protect, defend, hedge in." Lucifer was to protect the glory of God, which he reflected.

The first seeds of iniquity were sown in the holy mountain. Rebellion began ever so small. As the host of heaven worshiped God, Lucifer felt the first twinges of pride. Why, there was no one in heaven who could compare to him in beauty, wisdom, and skill! Or so he thought. He failed to realize that his source of splendor was rooted in the anointed light of God's glory. Without that illumination, his brilliance would abruptly fade into nothingness.

As Lucifer allowed the deception of pride to enter, mutiny against God was conceived. He began to say in his heart, *"I will ascend into heaven, I will exalt my throne above the stars of God: I will sit also upon the mount of the congregation, in the sides of the north: I will ascend above the heights of the clouds; I will be like the most High."*[24] No longer content to minister as the anointed cherub, he desired to ascend into heaven and to be like God.

The power of deception grew so greatly within Lucifer that he persuaded one-third of the angels to follow him.[25] In his attempt to destroy God, Lucifer's proud ambitions filled him with violence. *"By the multitude of thy merchandise they have filled the midst of thee with violence, and thou hast sinned."*[26] Jesus explains the depth of Lucifer's malevolence in John 8:44. *"Ye are of your father the devil, and the lusts of your father ye will do. He was a MURDERER from the beginning, and abode not in the truth, because there is no truth in him. When he speaketh a lie, he speaketh of his own: for he is a liar, and the father of it."*

Pride over outward appearance birthed deception, iniquity, and violent rebellion against God. *"Thine heart was lifted up because of thy beauty, thou hast corrupted thy wisdom by reason of thy brightness: I will cast thee to the ground, I will lay thee before kings, that they may behold thee.* "[27] In Luke 10:18, Jesus recounted the outcome of Lucifer's foolish attempt to unseat God, *"I beheld Satan as lightning fall from heaven."* He was cast as profane out of the mountain of God. The end result of Lucifer's pride was destruction.

The expulsion of Lucifer left a vacancy in the heavenly realm. There was no one to reflect the glory. Who would replace Lucifer as the worship leader and reflector of God's glory? Would God appoint Gabriel or Michael to occupy this position of ministry? What would God create to fill this role?

"So God created man in his own image, in the image of God created he him; male and female created he them."[28] God did not choose to bring into being another angel in the image of Lucifer. An earthen vessel created in His own image would reflect God's glory.

Unable to destroy God, Lucifer continually seeks to destroy God's image and to replace it with his own. Music and pride in the outward appearance became the perfect weapons to use in the destruction of mankind. That is why true holiness, which encompasses our outward appearance and inward attitudes, is of such importance. A constant battle is being waged to control these areas of our lives. The prince of darkness desires to destroy every vestige of God's reflective light. The Church must recognize satan's strategy lest we fall prey to his diabolical machinations.

Jesus portrays the purpose of God's people in Matthew 5:14-16. *"Ye are the light of the world. A city that is set on an hill cannot be hid. Neither do men light a candle, and put it under a bushel, but on a candlestick; and it giveth light unto all that are in the house. Let your light so shine before men, that they may see your good works, and glorify your Father which is in heaven."* We are the source of spiritual illumination in a dark world, a beacon guiding people to God. With sin abounding on every side, we have been commanded to let our light shine. Our good works, namely a godly, separated lifestyle, result in God being glorified in us and through us.

The wondrous privilege of worshiping the Creator and reflecting His glory was taken from the "Son of the Morning" and bestowed upon the "Sons of God". *"That ye may be blameless and harmless, <u>the sons of God,</u> without rebuke, in the midst of a crooked and perverse nation, <u>among whom ye shine as lights in the world</u>."*[29] The sons of God have become the illuminators of God's glory in a world darkened by Lucifer's control. Let your light shine, never hide it under a bushel, and "don't let satan blow it out!!"

<u>Chapter Two Footnotes</u>:

1. Isaiah 44:6, 46:9-10
2. II Corinthians 4:18
3. Job 38:7
4. Daniel 8:15-27, 9:20-27
5. Luke 1:5-38
6. Revelation 12:7-12
7. Strong's Concordance, Hebrew and Chaldee Dictionary No. 1966
8. Ezekiel 28:12
9. Ezekiel 28:13
10. John 4:24
11. Exodus 33:20
12. Luke 24:39
13. John 5:37
14. John 1:18
15. I Timothy 6:16
16. II Chronicles 6:18

17. Acts 17:28
18. Psalm 104:1-2
19. I John 1:5
20. I Timothy 6:16
21. Acts 9:3
22. Revelation 21:23
23. Ezekiel 28:14 & 16
24. Isaiah 14:13-14
25. II Peter 2:4, Jude 1:6, Revelation 12:4
26. Ezekiel 28:16
27. Ezekiel 28:17
28. Genesis 1:27
29. Philippians 2:15

It All Starts
at the Top

How does the Church begin to fulfill this anointed place of ministry? Let us turn to the Scriptures to find the answer. The anointing oil was always poured on the head and flowed down to the skirts of the garments. King David wrote, *"It is like the precious ointment upon the head, that ran down upon the beard, even Aaron's beard: that went down to the skirts of his garments."*[1] In the same manner, the reflection of God's glory begins at the top and flows downward. The question of hair length has been covered in depth in previous books;[2] however, we will continue to explore some other aspects of this multi-faceted truth.

"So God created man in his own image, in the image of God created he him; <u>male and female created he them.</u>"[3] When God created mankind, He ordained the distinction of sexes. The man was to be a reflection of

God's image while the woman would be a reflection of the Church, God's bride.

Apostle Paul stated in I Corinthians 11:7, *"For a man indeed ought not to cover his head, forasmuch as he is the image and glory of God: but the woman is the glory of the man."* The masculine characteristics of a man are actually a representation of God's glory. Conversely, the feminine attributes of a woman are a glory to the man, who represents God. This mirrors the way the Church glorifies God through obedient submission to His Word.

As Paul deals with the subject of God's order in I Corinthians 11, he addresses the question of hair length. Hair length and style has continually been a major source of identity for both men and women. Short hair or the uncovered head identifies men while long hair or the covered head characterizes a woman's feminine appearance.

In his attempt to destroy God's image, satan has attacked the roles that were ordained for men and women. In the destruction of this vital area, God's image and eternal plan are distorted. As these roles become convoluted, it is increasingly difficult to tell who is who. Men sport ponytails and braids while women have masculine haircuts. The onset of "unisex" clothing and hairstyles should not be considered innocent. A hidden agenda is behind it all–the eradication of God's image.

Our hair is indicative of our relationship with God, portraying submission or rebellion. Lucifer, having been the "covering" cherub at one time, realizes completely the significance of the covered and uncovered heads. In light of this, the Church must seek to protect the power that God has invested in us. The darker the night, the brighter the light of God's glory will shine forth as we reveal His likeness in the earth. We must beware of any action on our part that would distort the reflection of God's glory.

The question has been asked in discussions about hair length, "Am I permitted to dye my hair?" Should you alter God's glory in this manner? Once again we go to the Word of God to find the answer to these complex questions.

King David declared, ***"For thou hast possessed my reins: thou hast covered me in my mother's womb."***[4] This Scripture tells us that God is creatively and actively involved in the development of human life. The psalmist wrote, ***"Thy hands have made me and fashioned me: give me understanding, that I may learn thy commandments."***[5] As the Master Designer, He decided upon the unique characteristics of each person. He chose our personalities, facial features, and the color of our skin, hair, and eyes. We are the handiwork of God.

Jesus said, ***"Which of you by taking thought can add one cubit unto his stature?"***[6] All the mental concentration that you can muster will not make you any taller. In the same vein of thought, Jesus stated in an earlier passage, ***"Neither shalt thou swear by thy head, <u>because thou canst not make one hair white or black</u>."***[7] He is saying that it is humanly impossible to change the color of your hair because the roots will always retain their original color. It may be coated with hair dye; nevertheless, it has not been permanently modified. If you dye your hair, God's master design will be marred, altering His image in your life.

Questions we might ask ourselves concerning hair dye are, "Why would I want to dye my hair, and what is my motivation?" Does God have anything to say about white or silver hair? Turn to Proverbs 16:31, where the wise man Solomon wrote, ***"The hoary head is a crown of glory, if it be found in the way of righteousness."*** We know that the man's short hair and the woman's long hair are reflections of God's glory. However, this verse of Scripture tells us that as a person's hair whitens with age, it transcends to a new level of beauty, becoming a **crown** of glory. A crown is a royal headdress. Instead of cursing those white hairs, bless them. God is creating a royal headdress of glory upon your head.

Solomon declared in Proverbs 20:29, *"The glory of young men is their strength: and the beauty of old men is the grey head."* God says the gray head is a source of beauty. He designed the aging process so that your hair and skin color change together in order to produce a dignified beauty in your latter years. As you age, you become a greater reflection of the Ancient of days.

Twice in the Scriptures God allows us to have a glimpse of His personage. Daniel described Him, *"I beheld till the thrones were cast down, and the Ancient of days did sit, whose garment was white as snow, and the hair of his head like the pure wool: his throne was like the fiery flame, and his wheels as burning fire."*[8] John the Revelator declared, *"And in the midst of the seven candlesticks one like unto the Son of man, clothed with a garment down to the foot, and girt about the paps with a golden girdle. His head and his hairs were white like wool, as white as snow; and his eyes were as a flame of fire; And his feet like unto fine brass, as if they burned in a furnace; and his voice as the sound of many waters."*[9]

The hair color that God chose for Himself is white, symbolic of His total and complete purity. In like manner,

41

as your hair whitens with age, it symbolizes the purity of your faith that has been tried in the fire. You are an even greater reflection of God's glory and holiness in a dark world.

There are two things that you should never touch—God's vengeance[10] and glory.[11] If the glory of God is not handled properly, serious consequences are the outcome. When Lucifer ceased to protect the glory, he no longer reflected it. Let us vigilantly defend the glory resting on our heads, refusing to compromise in any area of consecration. May the anointing oil flow from our heads down to the skirts of our garments. It all starts at the top!

<u>Chapter Three Footnotes</u>:

1. Psalm 133:2

2. Suggested reading: *Power Before The Throne* by Ruth Rieder; *A Hair Short of Glory* by Penny Watkins; *My Hair, My Glory* by Juli Jasinski

3. Genesis 1:27

4. Psalm 139:13

5. Psalm 119:73

6. Matthew 6:27

7. Matthew 5:36

8. Daniel 7:9

9. Revelation 1:13-15

10. Deuteronomy 32:35; Proverbs 20:22, 24:29; Romans 12:19

11. Isaiah 42:8, 48:11; Acts 12:21-23; I Corinthians 1:29

Don't Veil
the Glory

"The first recorded use of makeup in Western cultures comes from Ancient Egypt."[1]   Thebes, an Egyptian city filled with witchcraft and prostitution, was renowned for its painted women. They used exotic eye makeup to intensify their sexual attraction and to aid in the art of seduction. Makeup was also used in idol worship to please the gods and to gain their attention. Egypt's influence continued through the centuries as various cultures imitated its practices.

Cosmetics remained synonymous with harlotry, idolatry, vanity, and deceit, causing religious groups such as the Puritans to staunchly forbid the use of face paint. In his 1616 *Discourse Against Painting and Tincturing*, Puritan Thomas Tuke warned, "A painted face is a false face, a true falsehood, not a true face." Women who painted usurped the divine order, taking "the pencil out of God's hand" as poet John Donne phrased. Indeed, some viewed the cosmetic arts as a form of witchcraft.

For the majority of the nineteenth century, face painting was prohibited among respectable people. To most Americans, the painted woman was simply a prostitute who brazenly advertised her immoral profession through rouge and kohl. Newspapers, tracts, and songs associated paint and prostitution so closely as to be a generic figure of speech. In New York, "painted, diseased, drunken women, bargaining themselves away," could be found in theaters while in New Orleans, "painted Jezebels exhibited themselves in public carriages" during Mardi Gras. How did this sign of disrepute become the daily routine of millions?

The wall of resistance showed a few hairline cracks with the onset of theatrical influence. By the 1880s, Lillie Langtry, Adelina Patti, and other performers appeared in cosmetics advertisements and testimonials. Makeup slowly began to merge from the stage into everyday life, heightening the importance of image making and performance. Standardized models of beauty were introduced using photographic and stage makeup techniques that challenged the "natural" look. However, it would be several more years before society would accept makeup as the "norm."

Before World War I, painted women remained spectacles to a significant extent. "I have seen women going along the street with their cheeks aglow with paint, everyone twisting their necks and looking," one woman observed. Working women were sent home for appearing on the job with an "artificial complexion"; the manager of Macy's fired one rouged saleswoman in 1913 with the comment that "he was not running a theatrical troupe but a department store." Public authorities tried in vain to preserve the older ideal of womanly beauty. In 1915, a Kansas legislator proposed to make it a misdemeanor for women under the age of forty-four to wear cosmetics "for the purpose of creating a false impression." Several years later, policewomen in Newark collared teenage girls at the train stations, "overawed them by a display of their police badges, and forced them to wash rouge and powder from their faces." Juvenile courts granted parental requests to bar their delinquent daughters from making up. In these circumstances, paint still implied sexual enticement and trickery, a false face.

Men in particular maintained these conventional views. Edward Bok, editor of the *Ladies Home Journal*, observed in 1912 that men continued to see rouge as a mark of sex and sin: "The stigma has never been removed by men, and is not, in their minds today." Letters to the *Baltimore Sun* from male readers confirm his observation of that era's masculine mind-set. "Such decorating is the same as an invitation to a flirtation," one man stated flatly. "Every painted or flashily dressed woman is deemed by most men to be of questionable character." In an expanding consumer culture, these small goods posed yet another danger. One Evansville, Indiana, man sued for divorce, claiming his wife spent eighteen dollars monthly on cosmetics and perfume; another denied responsibility when his wife charged $1,500 for toiletries on their store account, saying she was "possessed of a passion for such luxuries."

Max Factor, a prominent makeup artist for movie stars, began to package his products and sell them out of his makeup studio. Others joined in this avenue of money making. Women such as Elizabeth Arden and Helena Rubinstein opened beauty salons on Fifth Avenue in New York City. Then smaller operations sprang up across the country. The initial products promoted were skin care systems that included an array of cleansing and nourishing creams for the face and neck.

After World War I, women's growing acceptance of

beautifying products blossomed into a mass market for cosmetics. From expensive skin creams to dime store makeup, new goods made their way into the marketplace as profits soared. Many major women's magazines partook of this new source of revenue by participating in advertisement. The promise of substantial proceeds caused former convictions about this questionable practice to be discarded. By the 1930s, regular beauty columns were standard fare as editors eagerly cooperated with the largest cosmetic firms.

With the inception of mass marketing, an advertising frenzy ensued as women were slowly being conditioned to believe that painting was permissible. Cosmetic ads endlessly reminded women that they were on display and must ever remain a vision of perfect beauty. The painted face had suddenly become the sign of the times. What had once been denounced as paint was now celebrated as *glamour*!

Thanks to Hollywood, cosmetics evolved into the giant industry it is today. During the twenties, makeup features in magazines were rare. Today movie stars appear in fan and fashion magazines, contributing to the new looks with their step-by-step guides. With the help of face makeup, eye shadows, pencils, mascara, rouge, and the very essential lipstick, the "girl next door" can become a "glamour girl".

Ironically, vanity, deceit, and desire, having once been seen as women's vices, were now considered signs of a normal mind. Beauty manuals and women's magazines urged women to encourage narcissism in their daughters. Asserting women's "right to ROMANCE", advertisements offered cosmetics as talismans and weapons in the proper quest for men and marriage. "Most men are like babies," stated one beauty guide, and women should use cosmetics to manipulate them–discreetly.

In the 1920s and 1930s, cosmetics producers, beauty experts, and advertisers shifted the burden of female identity from an interior self to a personality made manifest by marking and coloring the face. They claimed makeup was a true expression of feminine identity and not a false mask. Making over was a means of individual self-development. Underlying all the skillful advertising techniques and high-sounding ideals was a prevailing lust for money. Women were brainwashed into believing that beauty could be found in a bottle of makeup.[2]

What started as a cry for liberation and a bid for freedom from restraints has in fact become an instrument of bondage. Women are coerced to believe that they are not beautiful without makeup. They are afraid to perform the smallest tasks outside their homes unless they have put on their "face". Self-confidence is destroyed incessantly as one beauty ideal after the other assaults women.

It is interesting to note that makeup was originally used to advertise harlotry. However, ambitious entrepreneurs and beauty experts strive to prove and proclaim its respectability while at the same time they are concealing its primary purpose. "Female makeup is conventionally thought of as a means of disguising age and imperfections. In fact, it only does this partially; its main effect is to create the appearance of erotic arousal: the wide eyes, the swollen, reddened lips, the flushing of the skin."[3] Once again, the cover-up is exposed. Considering the weight of this disclosure, is makeup really innocent after all?

Modern stores are filled with beauty aids of every sort. There are paints for faces, fingers, and feet. If a person is not content with her appearance, she can have a makeover! The latest craze is tattooed makeup. A woman no longer needs an hour to put on her "face". She can wear rouge, eye shadow, and lipstick permanently. A remedy is even offered for tattered fingernails! Just visit a salon to have fake nails applied. Talk about convenience!

Magazines are full of advertisements and articles

detailing the most fashionable grease paint and fingernail polish colors. Women are enticed to paint their face, fingers, and toe nails in the most hideous colors, all in the name of beauty. Meanwhile, the Church does not remain immune to these voices.

The enemy whispers in our ears that indulging in these fashions will not hurt us. "Just take a little bite of the forbidden fruit. After all, who wants to look pale as a ghost or have washerwoman hands?" **STOP!!** Before you buy into his lies, let us unmask the origin of the art of artifice. Is it okay to make up? Should we turn a blind eye to the worldliness that is creeping in, or is it time to sound an alarm? Should the children of God who are called to reflect His glory engage in such practices? Let us find out what the Word of the Lord says to us concerning these matters.

Lucifer was created perfect in beauty.[4] As he reflected the light of God's glory, he was the epitome of flawless perfection. However, his separation from God obliterated all traces of his previous splendor. No longer the shimmering, anointed cherub, Lucifer became darkness, the direct opposite of the light he once radiated. Isaiah prophesied, *"They that see thee shall narrowly look upon thee, and consider thee, saying, Is this the man that made the earth to tremble, that did shake kingdoms; That made the world as a wilderness, and destroyed the cities thereof; that opened not the house of his prisoners?*"[5]

No longer the magnificent creature he once was, Lucifer must resort to subterfuge in order to enhance his appearance. The initial guise that he assumed was that of a serpent in the Garden of Eden. His first order of business was to annihilate God's creation to gain control of the earth.

Through his subtlety satan beguiled Eve, convincing her God had created mankind imperfect. Partaking of the forbidden fruit would open their eyes, making them like gods, knowing good and evil. Eve thought God's image would be greatly enhanced when in reality it was soon to be destroyed.

Satan's strategy has not changed. He continually tells mankind their lives will be improved by partaking of what he offers. In his quest to destroy God's image, the devil assumes many disguises. He masquerades as a beast, a dragon, the Anti-Christ, and the False Prophet.[6]

Peter warned us, *"Be sober, be vigilant; because your adversary the devil, as a roaring lion, walketh about, seeking whom he may devour."*[7] Who is the true lion–the Lion of the tribe of Judah? Satan is bold enough to pose as the Son of God while seeking to devour an unsuspecting soul through false doctrine.

Paul spoke of satan's ability to transform himself, *"And no marvel; for Satan himself is transformed into an angel of light."*[8] Although he appears as a light bearer, in reality his light is darkness. Jesus averred, *"If therefore the light that is in thee be darkness, how great is that darkness!"*[9] Lucifer is the greatest makeup artist who ever existed!

Consider for a moment the words "makeup" and "made-up". These words are used to depict something that is false. When someone tells a lie, we say, "He made that up," or "She makes it up as she goes along." That is why we do not make up. Because *"no lie is of the truth"*![10]

Genesis 1:27 states that we are created in the image of God, the most extraordinarily beautiful Being that ever existed. If we are created in God's likeness, why would we want to alter His image? Yet satan tries to tell us that we would look better if we looked like him.

Throughout Scripture, makeup has always been synonymous with idolatry and harlotry. Jezebel was an extremely wicked woman whose influence contaminated both the nation of Israel and the nation of Judah. She sought to eliminate the worship of God through idolatry and whoredoms. Her idolatrous lifestyle included the practice of painting her face.[11]

The Old Testament records how Israel and Judah chose to follow the ways of the heathen. They began to worship their gods and engage in pagan rituals. As a result, God resolved to send them into captivity. Jeremiah and Ezekiel were sent to warn God's people of impending judgment. With picturesque language both prophets portray these backslidden nations as harlots with painted faces.[12]

The human face, which is created in God's image, is a mirror that reflects His glory to an idolatrous generation. This is illustrated beautifully in the life of Moses. For forty days and forty nights, Moses communed with the Lord on the top of Mount Sinai. *"And it came to pass, when Moses came down from mount Sinai with the two tables of testimony in Moses' hand, when he came down from the mount, that Moses wist not that the skin of his face shone while he talked with him."*[13] The glory of the Lord emanated from Moses' face as a radiant testimony of his glorious experience.

Remembering the circumstances surrounding Moses' previous trek down the mountain, Aaron and the children of Israel were afraid to come near. Aaron had made a golden calf for the people to worship. With reckless abandon, they had stripped off their clothes to indulge in unspeakable heathenish rites, provoking God's wrath that threatened to completely exterminate them. When the Israelites beheld the glory of God shining upon the face of Moses, it reminded them of their sin. At their request, Moses wore a veil whenever he spoke with them.

Likewise, when our lives are transformed by the power of God's Spirit, glory is revealed in our faces. The glory of God intimidates when we walk through the midst of this wicked and perverse generation. The world wants us to veil the glory so they will not be reminded of a holy God who judges sin.

In II Corinthians 3 the apostle Paul writes about this incident in the Old Testament. *"But if the ministration of death, written and engraven in stones, was glorious, so that the children of Israel could not stedfastly behold the face of Moses for the glory of his countenance; which glory was to be done away: How shall not the ministration of the spirit be rather glorious? For if the ministration of condemnation be glory, much more doth the ministration of righteousness exceed in glory."*

As Paul draws the parallel between the two covenants, he focuses on the revelation of the glory in the face of Moses. That glory was transient; however, the radiant power of the Spirit will never fade. *"Now the Lord is that Spirit: and where the Spirit of the Lord is, there is liberty."* We have been liberated from the power of darkness, and that liberty shines forth in the unveiled faces of the saints of God.

"But we all, with open face beholding as in a glass the glory of the Lord, are changed into the same image from glory to glory, even as by the Spirit of the Lord."

The glory of God can only reflect in a face free of deception. We do not need any cosmetics to enhance our appearance. The only beautifying agent that a saint of God needs is the Holy Ghost; *"he will beautify the meek with salvation."*[14]

Can Max Factor, Maybelline, or Revlon compete with God's beauty technique? Do not fall prey to the enemy's lies. Don't ever veil the glory!

Chapter Four Footnotes:

1. The Body Shop Team, *The Body Shop Book: Skin, Hair and Body Care* (New York, Penguin Group, 1994) page 63

2. All other cosmetic research excerpted from:
   A. *Hope in a Jar/The Making of America's Beauty Culture*, Kathy Peiss (Metropolitan Books, Henry Holt and Company, Inc., 1998)
   B. *Fashions of a Decade, The 1930's*, Maria Costantino (Facts on File 1992)

3. *The Language of Clothing*, Alison Lurie (Vintage Books, A Division of Random House, New York) page 237

4. Ezekiel 28:12

5. Isaiah 14:16-17

6. Revelation 11:7, 12:3-9, 13:11-15, 20:10; I John 4:3; II Thessalonians 2:3-4

7. I Peter 5:8

8. II Corinthians 11:14

9. Matthew 6:23

10. I John 2:21

11. II Kings 9:30

12. Jeremiah 4:30, Ezekiel 23:40

13. Exodus 34:29

14. Psalm 149:4

All That Glitters Is Not Good

Has the gleaming glint of precious stones ever captivated you? Have you been enticed to stop and peer through the jeweler's window? From childhood I seemed to gravitate toward the glitter. My spiritual struggle was not with cutting my hair or wearing makeup; rather, I was fascinated with sparkling jewels. Never owning a necklace or a pair of earrings, I learned many ways to adorn myself with "legal" jewelry. Before long my wardrobe was filled with button covers, shoe clips, brooches, pearl studded shoes, bejeweled clothing, and hair jewelry of every sort. If an outfit did not have enough sparkle, I added more. Gradually, the desire for glitter consumed me as I began creating outfits filled with gold, pearls, and bright baubles.

Meanwhile, the Lord started dealing with my desire howbeit the spiritual wake-up call was none too pleasant. As the Holy Ghost convicted me, I grew very defensive.

The Lord was patient with me and continued to whisper to my heart in a still, small voice. After several months, I began to respond to His voice.

One incident in particular comes to mind. Invited to attend a Gideon banquet that honored ministers and their wives from several denominations, I donned a gold sweater covered with gold bars and amber diamonds. Catching a glimpse of myself, a dart of conviction smote my heart. My outfit shimmered more than any other woman's jewelry in the room. At that point I realized that my clothing did not glorify God; it drew attention to me.

Slowly responding to the voice of God's Spirit, I reached the day when I could surrender this area of my life to God. Over a process of time, my life was cleansed and liberated from this worldly desire. Much later my understanding would be opened concerning the spiritual struggle I had passed through.

Precious stones beckon and allure. Calling attention to the person wearing them, they foster a spirit of vanity. Where did these sparkling jewels originate, and why did God create them? ***"Thou hast been in Eden the garden of God; every precious stone was thy covering, the sardius, topaz, and the diamond, the beryl, the onyx, and the jasper, the sapphire, the emerald, and the carbuncle, and*** *gold: the workmanship of thy tabrets and of thy pipes was prepared in thee in the day that thou wast created. "*[1]

Precious stones were initially created for the express purpose of reflecting God's glory. When Lucifer was cast as profane from the mountain of God, jewels ceased to be a medium whereby God reflected His glory. After his expulsion from Heaven, satan used jewelry to effect his influence in the earth.

Allow me to illustrate how it reveals his influence. Hurrying through the Dallas/Ft. Worth airport, I noticed a woman who appeared to be a sister in the Lord. Preparing to greet her, I stopped short upon catching sight of earrings dangling from her ears. Pierced ears identified her allegiance and revealed the influence that held sway in her life.

During a visit to an antique store while on a trip to Santa Fe, I saw a woman on a couch, talking to herself. Muttering to the pillow beside her, she was dressed in the most bizarre fashion. Bracelets lined her arms and legs, earrings filled her ears, and a multitude of necklaces draped her neck. Jewelry covered her head; numerous chain belts hung around her waist. When my husband drew near, the spirits that possessed her became visibly agitated. What a tragedy to see a life tyrannized by demon possession! This woman was enslaved by the devil, and her captivity was disclosed in the magnitude of jewelry that she wore.

Jewelry nourishes the spirit of pride, drawing attention to the flesh. I learned firsthand how easy it is to become ensnared by its enticing beauty. Jewelry is one of the tactics satan employs to gain control of our lives. Because we are reflectors of God's glory, removing all traces of the enemy's influence from our lives is essential. Then and only then can the brilliance of God's Spirit shine through unhindered.

Precious stones will never be used again to reflect the glory. They are simply building materials for the construction of the New Jerusalem. The prophet Malachi identifies who will reflect God's glory throughout all eternity. *"Then they that feared the LORD spake often one to another: and the LORD hearkened, and heard it, and a book of remembrance was written before him for them that feared the LORD, and that thought upon his name. And they shall be mine, saith the LORD of hosts, in that day when I make up my jewels"!!*[2] The saints of God will radiate God's splendor forever and ever when His glory is revealed in us. Now that's good glitter!

<u>Chapter Five Footnotes</u>:

1. Ezekiel 28:13
2. Malachi 3:17

Temples of Glory

Moral decay is rampant, and the spirit of sensuality holds sway in our society. Nudity has become commonplace as the fashion industry systematically churns out provocative apparel that seduces and appeals to the lust of the flesh. What would have been deemed scandalous attire a few, short years ago is now run-of-the-mill. How did this come about?

The process of desensitization did not happen in one days' time. It has taken over two centuries to demolish the walls of conservatism in clothing. Throughout the eighteenth and nineteenth centuries, apparel remained modest for both men and women. Styles changed from time to time, but skirts stayed ankle or floor length for women. A woman who showed her ankles was considered a loose woman.

Men's and women's clothing continued to show marked distinction in their characteristics. Women always wore dresses while men wore trousers. It was unthinkable to even conceive of a woman's wearing men's attire. Nevertheless, in 1850 the first assault was made on the conventional dress code as feminists dared to wear trousers beneath short dresses. These garments were dubbed "bloomers" after feminist editor Amelia Bloomer. America was not quite ready for such a radical departure from traditional values, and a public outcry ensued. For the time being, Turkish trousers on women remained unacceptable; however, the idea had been broached. Next time, people would not be so violently opposed.

In 1890 Charles Dana Gibson, a cartoonist, created the likeness of a beautiful woman that epitomized the Victorian feminine ideal. An all-American icon, the "Gibson Girl" would retain popularity for over twenty years. During the same decade, another attempt was made to introduce more masculine clothing for women. The new fashion designed for female bicyclists was called the "divided skirt". Public outrage was not as great over this tangent, and eventually the style was generally accepted.

Skirts remained long and hats large though makeup was virtually nonexistent at the onset of the twentieth century. Fashions were relatively unchanged until the revolution and rebellion of the Roaring Twenties. Several factors contributed to the fanatical deviation from previous feminine behavior and attire.

First, "actresses and professional beauties were no longer seen as women of questionable morality, but rather as celebrities and stars."[1] Women began to emulate their makeup, hairstyles, and fashions. They imitated women such as "Vampire" Theda Bara, the original sex goddess, who seduced and ruined men. She was famous for her seductive clothing, hypnotic kohl-rimmed eyes, and heavy barbaric looking jewelry. Actors and actresses heavily influenced behavior and fashions. This trend would persist with the onset of Hollywood and larger than life movie stars.

The passage of women's suffrage also had a terrific bearing on the female mind-set. Suddenly liberated from all former political restraints, women began casting their votes. Unfortunately, they cast aside their morals and virtues as well. The "flapper" openly necked in parked cars, smoked cigarettes, and danced the night away in roadhouses.

Another agent of change was the discovery of King Tut's tomb. Women painted their faces and cut their hair as they copied the fashions of Egypt. They wore Egyptian style tunics, slave bracelets, and serpent headbands. Ironically, in their quest for freedom, they actually adopted clothing that symbolized bondage.

Finally, the fourth major factor that contributed to moral demise was the First World War. "During the war years, fashions remained conservative, though skirts rose slowly from floor level to just above the ankle, easing the life of the many women now working outside the home or serving as nurses or members of the auxiliary corps. After peace broke out hems continued to rise rapidly."[2] Women seemed driven to break away completely from all former traditions as they bobbed their hair, wore short dresses, and openly painted their faces. Along with these revolutionary changes came the wearing of pants and shorts. The seeds that had been sown seventy years earlier with the intro-duction of "bloomers" finally blossomed into maturity.

The 1930s brought back longer skirts; however, another style was introduced at this time that would have a great bearing on future fashions. It was called the "cut up" skirt. Actresses such as blonde bombshell Jean Harlow, a famous sex symbol during the '30s, wore these cuts or "slits" to underscore her sex appeal. Clothing would never return to former levels of modesty as the '40s and '50s followed the fashion trends that were started in the '20s–short skirts, heavy makeup, and cut hair. During World War II, trousers became totally acceptable as a form of feminine attire while women progressed further in their quest for liberation and equality with men. Subsequent decades would reap a harvest of moral destruction from the seeds sown many years earlier.

The fashions of the '20s came full circle in the '60s, but this time the desensitizing process allowed for greater excess in nudity and sensuality. The '20s flapper with her mannish figure bobbed her hair, had kohl-rimmed eyes, and wore <u>knee grazing</u> dresses. The '60s ideal, embodied in Twiggy's boyish looks and stick thin figure, also had bobbed hair and kohl-rimmed eyes. However, she took clothing to a new level of immodesty with the inception of the <u>miniskirt</u>. While the flappers openly necked in parked cars, smoked cigarettes, and danced the night away in roadhouses, the children of the '60s and '70s would become involved with psychedelic drugs, marijuana, love-ins, and nudist colonies. The sexual revolution that began forty years earlier bore bitter fruit, resulting in the complete destruction of moral values.

Avant fashion designers such as Rudi Gernreich "continued to design articles of clothing intended to chisel away at the national prudery."[3] He generated styles such as the topless bathing suit in 1964, see-through blouses, and mini dresses inset with clear vinyl strips. The "cut up" skirt of the 1930s resurfaced as skin revealing slits in the midi skirt. Popular new fashions such as bikinis, hot pants, and halter tops swept the marketplace as modesty exited out the door, and the country perpetuated its downward spiral. As inhibitions were consistently lowered, people grew accustomed to exposing their flesh.

THE MORAL DESTRUCTION OF A NATION WAS REVEALED IN THE CLOTHING WORN BY ITS CITIZENS!! "As James Laver has remarked, modes are but the reflection of the manners of the time." Likewise, the moral condition of the Church will be manifested by the styles that are adopted and embraced by its constituents. Clothing is merely an outward indication of an inward condition. "Clothing is inevitable. They are nothing less than the furniture of the mind made visible."[4]

For thousands of years, human beings have been communicating with one another in the language of dress. Long before I am near enough to talk to you on the street, in a meeting, or at a party, you announce your sex, age, and class through what you are wearing. Important information (or misinformation) as to your occupation, origin, personality, opinions, tastes, sexual desires, and current mood is conveyed by your attire. I may not be able to put into words what I observe, yet the information is registered subconsciously. By the time we meet and converse, we have already spoken to one another in an older and more universal tongue–the language of clothes.[5]

God understood the communication of clothing from the beginning. This concept is illustrated perfectly in the story of Adam and Eve. God formed Adam from the dust of the ground, placed him in the Garden of Eden, and created Eve to be a helpmeet for him. When God brought the first man and woman together, the Scripture says, *"And they were both naked, the man and his wife, and were not ashamed."*[6]

In their state of innocence, shame was nonexistent between the first couple. Seduced by the serpent, Adam and Eve ate of the forbidden fruit, and sin intruded paradise. Purity of heart was shattered. *"And the eyes of them both were opened, and they knew that they were naked; and they sewed fig leaves together, and made themselves aprons."*[7]

The first repercussion of the fall of man was the awareness of nakedness. In the wake of disobedience, Adam and Eve constructed the first clothing of fig leaves. Nevertheless, their manmade aprons were insufficient, so God replaced the fig leaves sewn by Adam and Eve with a proper covering. *"Unto Adam also and to his wife did*

the LORD God make coats of skins, and clothed them."[8]
The Hebrew word for "coats" is **kuttoneth** (pronounced
koot–to'–neth), meaning a coat, garment, or robe to cover.
God made coats that covered the nakedness of Adam and
Eve, thereby setting forth a divine precept of modesty for
mankind. Lust had gained admittance into the world, so
humanity could no longer walk about unclothed because
the destruction of innocence necessitated the covering of
nakedness.

The erroneous argument that God is not concerned
about the kinds of clothes people wear has absolutely no
foundational support in Scripture. He cared enough to
provide proper attire for the first man and woman! This
account clearly demonstrates God's criteria for clothing;
He ordained that mankind should be properly covered.

Modesty cannot be defined by the current societal
ideals. As the preceding historical commentary demonstrates, society has diminished and even eliminated former
clothing restraints. God's Church must be governed by the
guidelines outlined in His Word. These precepts never
change as the psalmist declared in Psalm 119:89 and 142,
*"For ever, O LORD, thy word is settled in heaven. Thy
righteousness is an everlasting righteousness, and thy
law is the truth."*

Desensitization by the current culture has allowed carnal clothing to creep into the Church. It is common-place today to attend the House of God and see openly exposed thighs and vulgar, skin tight apparel that is sexually provocative. The young and old freely wear clothing that reveals their flesh as the spirit of sensuality invades the Church.

A look at history confirms that knee grazing skirts and long slits, popular styles freely worn among God's people, have their roots in rebellion and sexual enticement. When slits first invaded the Church, there was an uproar as we were told to sew them or pin them closed. However, over the process of time, people grew tired of addressing the issue, and slits crept higher and higher. At the same time, skirts have become shorter and shorter with the addition of indecent "cuts". These styles have frequently been defended as many declare that such clothing was acceptable in days gone by. Again, it is imperative that we understand that our standard of righteousness cannot be predicated upon the standard of the world. The Word of God is our only legitimate measuring rod.

His Word commands in Exodus 20:26, *"Neither shalt thou go up by steps unto mine altar, that thy nakedness be not discovered thereon."* God is adamant about modesty. He instructed His people not to make steps leading up to His altar because it was forbidden for their flesh to be exposed in the place of worship.

Isaiah 47:1-4 also clarifies how God views the uncovering of a woman's legs and thighs. *"Come down, and sit in the dust, O virgin daughter of Babylon, sit on the ground: there is no throne, O daughter of the Chaldeans: for thou shalt no more be called tender and delicate. Take the millstones, and grind meal: uncover thy locks, <u>make bare the leg, uncover the thigh</u>, pass over the rivers. <u>Thy nakedness shall be uncovered, yea, thy shame shall be seen</u>: I will take vengeance, and I will not meet thee as a man. As for our redeemer, the LORD of hosts is his name, the Holy One of Israel."*

In this passage of Scripture, the Lord is declaring vengeance on Babylon and Chaldea. God's judgment brought humiliation to the royal princesses, who were cast from their thrones. No longer women of refinement and dignity, they became slaves, exposing their flesh in the sight of common men.

Royal women of that day never exposed themselves in this manner. They wore veils and peered out of latticed windows.[9] The humiliation of nakedness was one of the greatest punishments that could be inflicted upon these delicate women. History verifies that nakedness was associated with slavery while proper clothing was a sign of royalty. In ancient Egypt, for instance, slaves and servants often wore nothing or, at most, a brief loincloth, but aristocrats put on clothes to indicate rank. Even in colder climates and more Puritanical societies, it has generally been true that the more clothes someone wears, the higher his or her status or position. This principle can be viewed in Medieval and Renaissance art. Peasants wore relatively few garments while kings and queens were burdened with layers of gowns, robes, and mantles even in indoor scenes.[10]

Indeed, the secular world recognizes the correlation between bondage and nudity. Furthermore, nakedness is a shame, as well as a sign of slavery, in God's sight. We are no longer enslaved by sin but have been made kings and priests unto God. The Church is spiritual royalty, a royal priesthood. Heaven's royal family should never expose their flesh in view of common man!

We have taught on the essentiality of women not wearing things that pertain to a man. However, a woman can wear a dress and be indecent or even vulgar. One fashion commentator noted, "Clothes that simultaneously conceal and reveal, and–like a half-opened gift– invite us to imagine what lies beneath, are traditionally erotic in their effect."[11] The peek-a-boo effect produced by the slit skirt is very seductive. Slits worn open to or above the knee expose the thighs when the wearer walks and climbs steps. Here is some food for thought. If you cut off your skirt where the slit ends, would you still be able to wear it?

Should a saint of God be seen in an outfit that is low cut, form fitting, and so revealing nothing is left to the imagination? Here is the message communicated by seductive apparel: "The garment that is partially unfastened not only reveals more flesh but implies that total nakedness will be easily achieved."[12] Is that what you want your clothes to imply? Does this sort of attire glorify God or entice the flesh? What kind of effect will it have upon men who are attracted by what they see?

Jesus addressed this situation in Matthew 5:27-29. *"Ye have heard that it was said by them of old time, Thou shalt not commit adultery: But I say unto you, That whosoever looketh on a woman to lust after her hath committed adultery with her already in his heart. And if thy right eye offend thee, pluck it out, and cast it from thee: for it is profitable for thee that one of thy members should perish, and not that thy whole body should be cast into hell."*

Under the Mosaic Law, the act of adultery was a sin punishable by death. However, New Testament grace is more demanding; looking and lusting constitute the sin of adultery. It would be easy to pass this off as being totally incumbent upon the men. Would that be fair?

Specific laws concerning adultery and rape are found in Leviticus 20:10 and Deuteronomy 22:22-29. A woman violated against her will was innocent. On the other hand, a woman who willingly participated in the adulterous act was held accountable and was put to death along with the man. If a woman wears clothing that incites a man to lust and commit adultery in his heart, she is also held accountable in the sight of God. If her pretty legs or attractive body outshine the light of the Holy Ghost, she has ceased to glorify God, and the Word asserts, *"That no flesh should glory in his presence."*[13]

Our brethren should not have to pluck out their eyes or take off their glasses because of the clothing that is being worn to the House of God. This world has become a flesh parade. The Church must be a sanctuary of holiness where we are not assailed by nakedness and fleshly lusts!

The issue of immodesty was not unfamiliar to the New Testament Church. They were surrounded by the Greek culture where nakedness was ordinary. "In ancient

Egypt, Crete and Greece the naked body was not considered immodest; slaves and athletes habitually went without clothing, while people of high rank wore garments that were cut and draped so as to show a good deal when in motion."[14] Paul alluded to the Olympian games and Grecian athletes in his writings. Clearly he was familiar with the heathen temples, rampant prostitution, nudity, and resulting moral decay in the Gentile society.

From this vantage point Apostle Paul addressed the issue of women's attire. ***"In like manner also, that women adorn themselves in modest apparel, with shamefacedness and sobriety; not with broided hair, or gold, or pearls, or costly array; But (which becometh women professing godliness) with good works."***[15] The word "modest" in the Greek is the word **kosmios** (pronounced *kos'–mee–os*). It means "orderly, decorous, of good behavior, modest." Decorous means "proper, seemly, correct." Women are being instructed to properly adorn themselves with appropriate attire in keeping with good behavior. Indecent clothing does not belong in the wardrobe of a godly woman.

Another key word in this Scripture is translated "shamefacedness". The Greek word is **aidos** (pronounced *ahee–doce'*). Its definition is "to have downcast eyes;

bashfulness towards men, modesty, awe towards God, reverence." There should be no brazenness in the actions of a godly woman. She is to be bashful or inclined to shrink from undue male attention. Modesty coupled with profound awe towards God govern a consecrated woman's conduct and clothing choices. She reverences her high calling as a holy woman, and this is displayed in her outward appearance.

One more word that describes the attire of a holy woman is "sobriety". That Greek word is **sophrosune** (pronounced *so–fros–oo'–nay*), meaning "soundness of mind, sanity, self control, soberness." In the fear of God, women should seriously evaluate the clothes they wear. What language is being spoken–the language of lust or the language of holiness? Self-control and clear thinking will enable a saint of God to choose garments that speak of godliness rather than worldliness.

It is interesting to note that the word "adorn" is used in this particular portion of Scripture. To adorn means "to beautify". God understands the woman's desire to be beautiful. He created them in this manner. Nevertheless, the secret to true and lasting beauty is found in adornment that is in keeping with the Word of God.

"What? know ye not that <u>your body is the temple</u>

of the Holy Ghost which is in you, which ye have of God, and ye are not your own? For ye are bought with a price: therefore glorify God in your body, and in your spirit, which are God's."[16] Paul likened the body of a believer to a temple. A temple is a building or place dedicated to the worship or the presence of a deity. The Greek word that was used for "temple" is **vaos**. This particular word refers to the Holiest of Holies where the shekinah glory of God dwelt. Our bodies have become God's dwelling place, a sacred inner sanctum filled with His glory. Since we belong to God, we cannot allow anything to defile this place of worship.

The High Priest approached the Holy of Holies very cautiously. Careful attention was given to every aspect of his appearance. He had to wear holy garments made of pure linen as he ministered before the Lord. This was a matter of life and death. Unholy attire was never permissible in the holy place because his vesture symbolized God's purity and the righteousness of the saints.

Likewise, our clothing should always exemplify holiness unto the Lord. Revelation 3:18 admonishes us to buy *"white raiment, that thou mayest be clothed, and that the shame of thy nakedness do not appear. . . ."* We cannot mix the sensual fabric of the world with the pure linen of righteousness. It could be a matter of spiritual life or death. ***"Know ye not that ye are the temple of God, and that the Spirit of God dwelleth in you? If any man defile the temple of God, him shall God destroy; for the temple of God is holy, which temple ye are."***[17]

As temples of glory dedicated to the worship of God, we cannot become desensitized by the licentious lifestyles that surround us. It is imperative that we keep our garments unspotted from the world. Non-believers are free to dress according to their own desires, but the children of God have been bought with a price. We are God's property, and He determines the manner in which we dress. ***"For ye are bought with a price: <u>therefore glorify God in your body</u>"!!***

Chapter Six Footnotes:

1. *Hope in a Jar/The Making of America's Beauty Culture*, Kathy Peiss (Metropolitan Books, Henry Holt and Company, Inc., 1998) page 48

2. *The Language of Clothing*, Alison Lurie (Vintage Books, A Division of Random House, New York) page 73

3. *New York Fashion, The Evolution of American Style*, Caroline Rennolds Milbank (Harry N. Abrams, Inc., Publishers, New York) page 223

4. *The Language of Clothing*, Alison Lurie (Vintage Books, A Division of Random House, New York) page 11

5. *The Language of Clothing*, Alison Lurie (Vintage Books, A Division of Random House, New York) page 3

6. Genesis 2:25

7. Genesis 3:7

8. Genesis 3:21

9. Genesis 24:65, Ruth 3:15, Song of Solomon 5:7, Judges 5:28

10. *The Language of Clothing*, Alison Lurie (Vintage Books, A Division of Random House, New York) page 120

11. *The Language of Clothing*, Alison Lurie (Vintage Books, A Division of Random House, New York) page 212

12. *The Language of Clothing*, Alison Lurie (Vintage Books, A Division of Random House, New York) page 231

13. I Corinthians 1:29

14. *The Language of Clothing*, Alison Lurie (Vintage Books, A Division of Random House, New York) page 212

15. I Timothy 2:9-10
16. I Corinthians 6:19-20
17. I Corinthians 3:16-17

Glorify God in Your Spirit

*"**F**or ye are bought with a price: therefore glorify God . . . in your spirit."*

Having seen how the glory of God is reflected in the outer man, let us focus on the reflection of God in the inner man. Holiness is much more than a list of guidelines that govern a person's outward appearance. Perfected holiness is depicted as a cleansing of the flesh and spirit. *"Having therefore these promises, dearly beloved, let us cleanse ourselves from all filthiness of the flesh and spirit, perfecting holiness in the fear of God."*[1] The weightier matters of the law such as judgment, mercy, and faith cannot be omitted from the equation of sanctification. If these components are absent, one's perspective of holiness can become convoluted and unbalanced, resulting in spiritual pride.

Obedience to God's Word must never become a

source of arrogance. The wise man Solomon admonished, ***"Only by pride cometh contention: but with the well advised is wisdom."*²** Conceit will cultivate judgmental, critical attitudes. Herein lies one of satan's most insidious although clever ploys. If he cannot persuade us to surrender our righteous lifestyle, he will tempt us to become proud in our piety. Pride furnishes fertile soil in which seeds of envy, strife, and debate will flourish. When these spirits gain control, true holiness no longer exists.

As a new convert, my husband Michael experienced firsthand the destructive effects of "spiritual" faultfinding. Thankfully, he survived, but how many others became casualties of criticism? Here is his story.

"I remember when I first came into the church in 1979. It was the greatest thing that ever happened in my life! I came out of the world in the days of John Travolta and Saturday Night Fever when disco was the rage. My usual dress was a tattered tee shirt and blue jeans. However, I became caught up in the disco craze, so I purchased white, high waisted, bell-bottom pants, a white vest, and a black shirt with a big collar. I also bought an awesome, crushed red velvet outift that had high waisted bell-bottom pants, a vest, and a wide collared pink shirt. Together with my black platform shoes, these were by far the best clothes

I owned.

"I was ready to hit the disco floor, but God decided it was time for me to hit the altar. He called me, He chose me, and He saved me. Praise God! Just four months after I obeyed Acts 2:38, camp meeting time came. I was ecstatic and couldn't wait to go! I got rid of my green Gideon Bible and purchased a new one bound in black leather. The only criteria in choosing my Bible was that it looked good at my side. As I packed for camp, it was obvious that my 'best' clothes must be included, so into the suitcase went my fancy duds and platform shoes. They were all I had besides blue jeans and tee shirts.

"Camp meeting was just like they said it would be. The choir sang like angels, and the preacher was on fire! I arrived early for every service so I could sit on the front row. As a new convert, I was drinking it all in and basking in the glow of my new, Holy Ghost filled life.

"And then it happened. . . . Following one of the services, I stood there in my freshly cleaned, crushed red velvet outfit, admiring all of God's wonderful people (a view made easier by the fact that my shoes made me three inches taller). Suddenly, two elderly women descended upon me, clothed in black from their chins to their wrists and to their ankles, the pictures of holiness from head to toe. They stopped in front of me and began staring and glaring, looking me up one side and down the other. Then with a 'Tsk, tsk,' they shuffled off with stern faces and critical eyes.

"Standing there in dazed shock, I wondered what I had done to deserve such castigating scowls. Up to that point, I had the newborn belief that Pentecostal saints could do no wrong, yet it was obvious that I did not meet with their approval. Two people who had no idea that I was only four months old in the Lord shattered me. All they knew was what I was wearing was too inappropriate for them.

"Why is it that the holier some people get, the more critical they become? Perhaps they have missed the point of what true holiness really is. Those two women could have destroyed my newfound faith with their judgmental attitudes. Like many others, I could have succumbed to the devil's lie that there is no love in the Church."

Maybe there is no love in some churches, and that is why they do not grow. There is no love in the world, and if there is no love in a church, that church is like the world –worldly. We are commanded, ***"Love not the world, neither the things that are in the world."***[3] Backbiting, backstabbing, envy, hatred, unforgivingness, jealousy, mercilessness, and pride are all in the world and are definitely not holy.

Jesus told a parable to certain people who trusted in their own righteousness and despised others. *"Two men went up into the temple to pray; the one a Pharisee, and the other a publican. The Pharisee stood and prayed thus with himself, God, I thank thee, that I am not as other men are, extortioners, unjust, adulterers, or even as this publican. I fast twice in the week, I give tithes of all that I possess. And the publican, standing afar off, would not lift up so much as his eyes unto heaven, but smote upon his breast, saying, God be merciful to me a sinner. I tell you, this man went down to his house justified rather than the other: for every one that exalteth himself shall be abased; and he that humbleth himself shall be exalted."*[4]

The publican went down to his house justified instead of the self-righteous Pharisee who thought he was the better man. Imagine that! The Lord justified the man with many faults rather than the man who thought he had few faults. If our fasting and tithing make us proud, our motives are wrong. If our holiness makes us haughty and we despise others, our intent is incorrect.[5]

James taught, *"Speak not evil one of another,*

brethren. He that speaketh evil of his brother, and judgeth his brother, speaketh evil of the law, and judgeth the law: but if thou judge the law, thou art not a doer of the law, but a judge. *⁶* The judgment seat may be the best seat in the house, but there is only One who is qualified to occupy that seat of power. **"There is one lawgiver, who is able to save and to destroy: who art thou that judgest another?"** *⁷*

Jesus rebuked the Pharisees and labeled them hypocrites for focusing on their outward appearance while ignoring the condition of their hearts. **"Woe unto you, scribes and Pharisees, hypocrites! for ye make clean the outside of the cup and of the platter, but within they are full of extortion and excess. Thou blind Pharisee, cleanse first that which is within the cup and platter, that the outside of them may be clean also."** *⁸* Outward holiness minus inward purity constitutes a Pharisee. It is possible to look good on the outside and be filthy inside. However, it is impossible to have true holiness on the inside without its shining gloriously on the outside.

Lucifer was the first one who was perfect in outward beauty, yet he was filled with deception and murder. Jesus warned us that appearances could be deceiving. **"Woe unto you, scribes and Pharisees, hypocrites! for ye are** *like unto whited sepulchres, which indeed appear beautiful outward, but are within full of dead men's bones, and of all uncleanness. Even so ye also outwardly appear righteous unto men, but within ye are full of hypocrisy and iniquity.*" You can look holy from head to toe and be nothing more than a hypocrite putting on a shallow display of insincere piety. A righteous exterior can actually disguise a repository of death filled with the remains of innocent victims who have been murdered by merciless gossip.

Paul emphasizes the proper attitudes for the inner man in Colossians 3:12-15. *"Put on therefore, as the elect of God, holy and beloved, bowels of mercies, kindness, humbleness of mind, meekness, longsuffering; Forbearing one another, and forgiving one another, if any man have a quarrel against any: even as Christ forgave you, so also do ye. And above all these things put on charity, which is the bond of perfectness. And let the peace of God rule in your hearts, to the which also ye are called in one body; and be ye thankful."* If we strive to put on these godly attributes, peace will rule in the Body of Christ.

The trumpet of truth must always sound a clear note; however, truth must be coupled with mercy. *"__By mercy__* *and truth iniquity is purged: and by the fear of the LORD men depart from evil.*"[10] The psalmist penned, *"Mercy and truth are met together; righteousness and peace have kissed each other."*[11] Judgmental, critical attitudes will destroy, but the truth spoken in love will produce the image of Jesus Christ in our lives and will bring increase to the body. *"But speaking the truth in love, may grow up into him in all things, which is the head, even Christ: From whom the whole body fitly joined together and compacted by that which every joint supplieth, according to the effectual working in the measure of every part, maketh increase of the body unto the edifying of itself in love."*[12]

Three times in the Word of God the Church is enjoined to worship the Lord in the beauty of holiness.[13] Many times this injunction is perceived as worshiping the Lord in the beauty of holiness "standards" such as long hair and dresses. However, to worship the Lord in the beauty of holiness literally means to worship the Lord in the beauty of being like Him.

The very nature of God is holiness. Moses spoke in worship, *"Who is like unto thee, O LORD, among the gods? who is like thee, glorious in holiness, fearful in praises, doing wonders?"*[14] In Isaiah 6:3 the seraphim cried, *"Holy, holy, holy, is the LORD of hosts."* God is the very essence of pure, unadulterated, holy beauty, and He commanded us, *"Be ye holy; for I am holy."*[15]

Holiness standards are a medium whereby we separate ourselves from the world and all its influences of evil. *"For ye were sometimes darkness, but now are ye light in the Lord: walk as children of light."*[16] As we are cleansed inside and out from the bondage of sin, the vestiges of satan's control are eradicated from our lives. This enables the image of God to shine forth and to reflect in the earth as we become holy even as He is holy.

Outward holiness standards by themselves will never save us. Obedience and submission to the Word of God bring salvation. This inward work of the Spirit is reflected in the outward appearance and actions of a true child of God. God is glorified in us as the beauty of Jesus is manifested in our bodies and spirits. May the words of this old hymn be our prayer. . . .

Let the beauty of Jesus be seen in me
All His wonderful passion and purity
O Thy Spirit divine all my nature refine
Till the beauty of Jesus be seen in me!

Chapter Seven Footnotes:

1. II Corinthians 7:1

2. Proverbs 13:10

3. I John 2:15

4. Luke 18:9-14

5. *Texico Trumpet*, May/June Issue, volume 49, #10

6. James 4:11

7. James 4:12

8. Matthew 23:25-26

9. Matthew 23:27-28

10. Proverbs 16:6

11. Psalm 85:10

12. Ephesians 4:15-16

13. I Chronicles 16:29; Psalm 29:2, 96:9

14. Exodus 15:11

15. I Peter 1:16

16. Ephesians 5:8

Chosen to Be Special

"For thou art an holy people unto the LORD thy God: the LORD thy God hath chosen thee to be a special people unto himself, above all people that are upon the face of the earth."[1]

The saga of God's chosen people begins with the calling of Abraham to a life of faith as recorded in Genesis 12. In time his beloved son Isaac was born, and the faith of Abraham was passed to the next generation. Isaac's eldest son Esau was next in line to receive God's special call. Unwisely, he despised the calling, selling it for a bowl of beans. As a result of Esau's choice to gratify his flesh and not his spirit, Jacob became the recipient of God's favor and blessing. *"As it is written, Jacob have I loved, but Esau have I hated."*[2]

Inherent in Abraham, Isaac, and Jacob was a

passionate devotion to Jehovah as they walked before Him in obedience. Because of the faithfulness of the patriarchs, God set His love upon Israel. *"The LORD did not set his love upon you, nor choose you, because ye were more in number than any people; for ye were the fewest of all people: But because the LORD loved you, and because he would keep the oath which he had sworn unto your fathers, hath the LORD brought you out with a mighty hand, and redeemed you out of the house of bondmen, from the hand of Pharaoh king of Egypt."*[3]

The chosen of God, Israel was favored above all people, obtaining the oracles of God. Nevertheless, Israel never comprehended the rare privilege she had been granted. Judges 5:8 says, *"They chose new gods."* A wandering eye of unfaithfulness led Israel to walk in the ways of the heathen and to embrace other gods. As a result, Israel committed spiritual adultery and disobeyed God's commands. Consequently, the Lord gave Israel a bill of divorcement.[4]

Israel's backsliding opened the door of blessing for you and me since God turned to the Gentiles to prepare a bride for Himself. *"But ye are a chosen generation, a royal priesthood, an holy nation, a peculiar people; that ye should shew forth the praises of him who hath called you out of darkness into his marvellous light: Which in time past were not a people, but are now the people of God: which had not obtained mercy, but now have obtained mercy.*"[5] Israel never cherished this wondrous election. Being the wild olive tree that was grafted in, we must never lightly esteem this incredible privilege. We are the Bride of Christ and have become the people of God.

Becoming a bride is one of the most exciting times in a woman's life. Once the proposal has been accepted and the date set, the planning begins. All the preparation only adds to the excitement of the bride; she spends hours looking through bridal magazines and visiting stores in order to find the perfect gown. At long last that special dress is purchased, along with the matching veil. Once pressed, it hangs in readiness, carefully protected from any possible damage; only the best dress will suffice.

Delighting in preparing herself for her groom, she dreams about walking down the aisle in her bridal attire. The lovely wedding dress is a daily reminder that soon she will be married to her beloved.

What an apt picture of the Church! We have been chosen as the Bride of Christ. The proposal was accepted when we repented, were baptized, and received the Holy Ghost. The date has been set, and God is preparing a place for us.

Meanwhile, the Bride is making herself ready. The wedding dress has been selected, and its description is found in Revelation 19:8. *"And to her was granted that she should be arrayed in fine linen, clean and white: for the fine linen is the righteousness of saints."*

Special care must be taken to insure the pristine condition of the wedding garment. Paul declared that God is returning for a glorious Church without *"spot, or wrinkle, or any such thing; but that it should be holy and without blemish."*[6] As a natural bride delights in her unique bridal attire, the Bride of Christ should delight in being set apart from the world. We are chosen of God and made special.

An interesting parable is found in Matthew 22, relating the wedding a certain king made for his son. This story contains powerful truths relevant to the Church.

"The kingdom of heaven is like unto a certain king, which made a marriage for his son, And sent forth his servants to call them that were bidden to the wedding: and they would not come. Again, he sent forth other servants, saying, Tell them which are bidden, Behold, I have prepared my dinner: my oxen and my fatlings are killed, and all things are ready: come unto the marriage.

But they made light of it. . . . And the remnant took his servants, and entreated them spitefully, and slew them. But when the king heard thereof, he was wroth: and he sent forth his armies, and destroyed those murderers, and burned up their city. Then saith he to his servants, The wedding is ready, but they which were bidden were not worthy. Go ye therefore into the highways, and as many as ye shall find, bid to the marriage. So those servants went out into the highways, and gathered together all as many as they found, both bad and good: and the wedding was furnished with guests. And when the king came in to see the guests, he saw there a man which had not on a wedding garment: And he saith unto him, Friend, how camest thou in hither not having a wedding garment? And he was speechless. Then said the king to the servants, Bind him hand and foot, and take him away, and cast him into outer darkness; there shall be weeping and gnashing of teeth."

Twice the Jewish nation was bidden to the wedding, yet they would not come. Riches and real estate were more important than responding to the wedding invitation. Slaying the messengers who summoned them to the feast brought destruction as the armies of Rome burned their city. Consequently, the King requested others to take the place of the unworthy guests.

God called the Gentiles to the marriage feast; the guests will be gathered from every walk of life, *"both bad and good."* After accepting the invitation, each person must prepare his or her wedding garment. The world loudly claims that separation and holy living are no longer an essential part of salvation. Deceived, they will seek to gain entrance to the marriage without proper attire.

When the King appears at the wedding feast, He will confront those who came in without a wedding garment. In spite of their loud boasting today, they will be speechless in that day. Bound hand and foot, they will be cast into outer darkness.

"For many are called, but few are chosen."

Israel spurned the wedding invitation and chose to follow the heathen nations surrounding her. What choices will the latter day Church make? Will we accept God's marriage proposal and choose the positive power of holiness, or will we follow the compromising course of worldliness? Will we reflect Lucifer's likeness or God's glory? Our choices will determine our destiny!

Which standard of beauty will you emulate? Will you opt for the world's version portrayed in the similitude of a painted prostitute complete with bobbed hair, Egyptian eyes, fake fingernails, painted toenails, jewelry, and seductive clothing? Or will you choose God's beauty ideal embodied in the form of a pure, chaste, virgin bride arrayed in fine, white linen, who reflects His glory on her head and face and in her body and spirit?

God will live with His wife for eternity, so He can afford to be choosy. His Bride will be chosen because she is set apart and special. Are you chosen to be special? The choice is up to you!!

"For he is Lord of lords, and King of kings:
and they that are with him are
called, and chosen, and faithful."[7]

Chapter Eight Footnotes:

1. Deuteronomy 7:6

2. Malachi 1:2-3, Romans 9:13

3. Deuteronomy 7:7-8

4. Isaiah 50:1, Jeremiah 3:8

5. I Peter 2:9-10

6. Ephesians 5:27

7. Revelation 17:14